Out of Nowhere

Poems
from the
Inward Journey

Out of Nowhere

Poems
from the
Inward Journey

Robert K. Hall

Running Wolf Press
Healdsburg, California

ISBN   0-9701333-2-4

Photography by Jan E. Watson
Book design: Chip Wendt
Cover design: Alvaro Colindres & Donna Schaffer
Printing: Barlow Printing, Cotati, California

Published by
Running Wolf Press
518 Johnson Street
Healdsburg CA   95448
MagusLudus@aol.com

For the people of Spirit Rock,
my first spiritual home

Foreward

"You can't get the news from poetry, but men and women die every day for lack of what is found there."
                                    --Wallace Stevens

   Robert's poems are plainspoken, plainsong, an invitation to the reality of the present. Usually we're lost in thought, oblivious, half asleep in habit. Then in some simple moment the song of a bird, the smell of coffee, a train whistle, our lover calling out our name, brings us back, here, alive. It is here that we touch the ordinary and the sacred, which is what Robert asks of us.
   Robert has been my good friend for more than a quarter century. He's led a fine dance, from Haight-Ashbury and Esalen, to India, Naropa and Spirit Rock; as a physician, healer, father, founder of one of the first schools of psychology to integrate body, psyche and spirit; mentor to hundreds, spiritual teacher to more. Finally, underneath all this, is a poet.
   His poems open the ears and the eyes, tell tender and honest truths to the soul. Their words come out of that spaciousness of meditation which rings of mystery. They join voices with the wisdom and ecstasy poems of Persia, India and Japan.
   A good poem is like wine, like a temple bell. Drink. Listen. Enjoy.

                              Jack Kornfield
                              Spirit Rock Center
                              Woodacre, California
                              June 2000

Preface

Meditation is a way of discovering who we *are* in truth, before the conditioned mind colors experience with opinions, judgements and agendas. Meditation allows us to view ourselves as innocents, naked in the middle of life.

These poems have all arrived on paper out of nowhere. Each one was written immediately after a period of meditation. They were caught in midair, so to speak. They were coaxed into existence out of a mind emptied, as much as possible, of analysis and conjecture.

They arrived spontaneously and were written down with little interference from the linear discursive thinker. Most of them have been examined many times for authenticity, sometimes edited slightly but mostly allowed to stand "as is."

The pieces in this little volume have been read aloud numerous times to meditation students in retreats, workshops and classes. I have selected these poems because they have made their home in the hearts and minds of many individuals who are finding their way on the inward path. My hope is they will be recognized as descriptions of way stations along the journey.

I offer them in the spirit of love.

Robert K. Hall

Contents

Foreward
Preface

The practice of meditation is certainly simple, but don't expect it to be easy. The discursive mind will inevitably answer our efforts to silence its random wanderings with ingenious challenges and obstacles.

It's Hard to Pick Your Way

It's hard to pick your way cleanly
through this magical forest.
There are so many trails and they
don't all lead to sunny meadows.

You have to lie down close to the
earth, on your belly, in the dirt,
press your cheeks to the reality of
it and listen with all your resolve.

Listen for the deep rumble that comes
from the molten center and gives
directions, pointers on what to watch
for and to how step carefully
through the brambles and
confusion of many voices, all talking
at once, until finally, a vast silence . . .

       not even birds dare to toss
       their sweet songs there

It's important to stop in one place
for a while, sit and count the
varieties of ferns and notice the
many colors of green. Do the
same thing over and over, as
though you must stand up, lie
down and stand up again in the
same way.

Burrow deep, always looking for
the life in your thoughts and
feelings. Sense the movement
around you and listen to leaves
shake in the raw wind.

Stay a while. Walk slowly and
don't be afraid to accumulate a
little dust on your shoes.

Love washes everything clean
                              in the end.

The Soldier

He stands inside my chest and throat,
a soldier at attention. Holding the
line, guarding the storehouse from
looters. They came once and stole
everything, every bit of trust, every
reassuring touch and all the spontaneity.

Those days were long ago, when
intruders came and left their bloody
footprints on my skin.
Still that soldier stands, holding a
musket, a feather in his hat.
I try to steal a smile from him
everyday, but he knows his duty.

I say, "At ease soldier! As you were
before strangers occupied the land,
as you were before my innocent
heart was cut open like a ripe melon!"

He guards the scars and every day I
visit with my bouquet of tender
attention, basket of appreciation.

We touch each other with understanding,
but he does not relax his stand for security.
He has his duties. I have mine.

The Skeptic

I'd like to believe we came from the Pleiades.
I'd love to belong to the stars and know
there is a journey back after the duty is done,
after light has won.

But when I look into memory or try to
reason this life into certainty, my mental
probe meets something like colorless soup,
no floating carrots, no celery, no tomatoes,
nothing that is anything, just blank
formless-no-admittance emptiness.

I don't know if I came from anywhere.
I can't remember going-away parties, or
good-byes. I just woke up here in terror, and
have been trying to find a map ever since.

Breaking Out

Some people take their clothes
off in public. I suppose you are
not one of those.

Rather, you perform your mating
ritual inside a deep closet of
dead trees.

Open the door!
Sin isn't always what people say.

Branches bloom when the wind
blows warm.

Out of Control

This thing is all out of control.
Doors slamming.
Window blinds slapping in the wind.
There is hardly a relaxed breath.

I'm trying to hold on to the
shoulders of this beast that is
galloping wildly and without
reason toward some distant
darkness where finally all the
separate parts, the arms and
knees and knuckles, will be
scattered into chaos,
total disorder.

Sound will roar in disembodied ears.
Trees will be whipped to the ground
just before the blast of light,
like a jewel glinting in the sun.

When all the effort to be a loveable
human being will cease, be
unnecessary, and there will be room
for every forbidden feeling, time for
every angry thought in one
final resting place.

The Ugly Truth

The truth is everybody has a
secret, stuff that will be revealed
not in this lifetime.

The self-contraction who
keeps secrets and longs for
legitimate existence will
never let the world know
how it picks its nose and
eats the product.

The self who never
confesses to touching its
own asshole in order to
bring the finger to the nose
and get ecstatic from the
smell of self.

There are some things the
small self will never do.

It will kill.
It will lie.
It will be betrayed.
It will cheat.

But it will never reveal how it
eliminates the whole world in order
to stay alive.

Our Friend Neurosis

Neurosis bites at your heels.
A reminder that fear
is the life style for you.

Never forget, you could be
abandoned any moment.
That little pain in your belly
is going to require surgery.

Everything you've worked for
will be meaningless
when everybody finds out about
your chocolate binges.

Maybe your mother did it.
Could be the first grade teacher
who made you empty the waste basket?

Every time someone smiles warmly
some muscle deep in your throat
contracts with apprehension.

Neurosis is so strong.
How could we live without it?
No drama makes for boring days.

Seeker's Song

There is no "I" down here,
only pretend.
There may be a "we,"
can't comprehend.

The thing is so strange,
always beyond us.
I'd like to give up, quit
making a fuss.

But somehow the searching
has a life of its own.
I'd like to lie down, reap the
seeds that I've sown.

I'm haunted by voices all
calling me back.
Remember the source while
under attack.

The pull is so strong I rarely can rest
from feeling the longing,
hoping the best.

Someday I'll be free to
dissolve into light.
That's what they say.
I'm hoping they're right.

In the meantime the problem
is how to spend time
when there's nobody *really* and I
still need a rhyme.

Let's do it together
join forces to love.
Maybe then the voices will call
like the dove.

Come home now my tender,
come home to your rest.
We've always been waiting,
come back to your nest.

Gathering Pieces

There are pieces of us scattered everywhere.
Maybe we should bring them in.

The 13-year old who stands hidden behind
a black curtain covered with black slime-shame.

The one who weeps, sits on the curbstone
grieving the gutters of city streets running
with swift dirty water.

The 9-year old whose head is bursting with
too much information.

Let's open our arms and make the gesture
of embracing all the lost fragments of our common life.
We have only to invite them in.
Encourage with gentle coaxing.

Whisper, *welcome,* in the night as our minds
open to the emptiness of our true condition.
So we can respond with gratitude
to the One whose fullness includes us all and
within whose loving heart all the scattered
pieces unite, come to rest.

Let's bring all the lost parts of
our childhood, all the hurt ones
who didn't understand their
wounds, together in this

time-body of flesh and bones.
Then we can sit and gaze on
the inner and outer worlds
without tearing ourselves into
separate parts ever again.

Call Off The Search

I walk upstairs.
I walk downstairs.
I wander into the kitchen
and look through a doorway into
the living room with all its books
and oriental carpets, but I can't
find the point of it all,
can't reach into what I'm looking
for until I sit down in the corner,
pull my blanket over my head,
close my eyes, look into the
interior rooms and listen for what
is moving in there, and again be
amazed that there is a river,
constant and uncreated, flowing,
announcing itself with the sound
of life everlasting, bursting into
this wrinkled brain substance,
translating itself into muscle,
bone, fat, connective tissue and dreams.

When I bathe in that immediacy,
I never have to search for
anything again.

Room for the Thief

Do we get to heaven when we don't follow the rules?
Is there room for the car thief and the con man?
What about illicit affairs and lusting for the forbidden?
Is there a place for defilements and purity too?

I want to know what the parameters are.
Just how serious is this business of Karma and debt?
My grandmother was a holy lover of the small and helpless,
but chopped the heads off chickens with her bloody axe.

This mind wonders on dusty trails and hidden canyons.
There are strategies and tricks no one would be proud of.
Feelings erupt. Pornographic shots of greed and
hatred insist on having their stage time.

I miss the message every day.
I sit still and hopefully chase awareness.
A chance to grab the golden ring
goes by every three seconds, yet
I still hear no angel choirs nor
have I ever sat on any golden throne.

Wide Open

Breath in. Breath out.
I like the cool-water-when-thirsty
feeling that comes with
open heart, clear passageways –
great ease of being.

When the dividing line
between the one who looks
at memory, contemplates
the future and the one not doing,
just feeling the river flowing,
gets clear, there is a vast difference
between one world and the other.

Who can describe that shift?
Not I. Nor anyone who writes.

Poems are just attempts at
telling somebody the futile,
but that's o.k.
Everyone who knows
always understands anyway.

I like that free feeling when
the line gets crossed from the
bondage of being somebody
into being wide open.

The Appearance of Things

Life is ordinary.
It happens all the time
without anyone doing anything.

What I'd like to know is
how that spark makes music,
or the symphony creates so
much solid soil, or how those
sterling roses grow out all lavender.

It's amazing that something
so light as vibration can solidify,
precipitate into bones, become
the form softer meat hangs on,
then expands and contracts to
make dance and drama.

Life is ordinary.
It happens all the time.
What we don't know is
what it is.

Portrait of the Individual Self

The "I" person exercises on cardiac machines.
The "I" person turns on the computer.
The "I" person wonders what needs to be done.
The "I" person is worried about duties.
The "I" person loves to think about himself.
             All this doing is exhausting.

The "I" person wonders if he could stop
for a while and see where everything comes from.
When he goes to sleep at night, vacation time
with no separations, no need to work at anything,
so refreshing. The "I" person can't help himself.
He has to do whatever he does when fear puts the
torch to his tenderness.

Now, while he is gone for a moment
let the voice of the great river
speak forth its joy of being here.
Look up and see through the
soul's window the light of empty sky
where there will be a piece of life with
wings and freedom cutting through air.

Now there is emptiness.
Vibration fills the universe and
echoes inside this head where the
"I" person makes his home.
He remembers he lives somewhere
and needs to do something.

The "I" person exists and doesn't exist
at the same time.
He tries to use logic for explanation,
but finds the age of reason has passed.

Rip Rap

This world is weird, isn't it?
Little kids shoot big guns,
killing other little kids and adults.

Whales escorted out to sea
with more care than me.

The beat goes on so fast you
have to tap dance or tie
yourself to the mast.

Everybody, every single
person, has some agenda other
people don't know about.

That means, we are all milling
around down here, bumping into
each other causing wounds, rather
than soothing our brother.

Nobody knows what's going
on, but lots of "big shots" talk
like they need to lead the pack
to the on-sale-rack where
money buys you what you
want as soon as you vote for
Mr. Fast Track.

We've got these bodies that

fade away, yet we never know
when comes the day, and no
matter how hard we work at
staying alive, everybody here
is destined to take that long
dive into ceasing and ending,
disappearing from sight.

Will someone tell me why we
put up such a fucking futile fight?

Technomadness

I'm going to kill my computer.
AOL is going to die, wither on
the vine, give up its last gasp
attempt to drive me insane.

I'm going to get it before it gets me.
There's no way some mechanical
monster brain, chaos frustration master
is going to make me as angry as I am.

I keep going back to its siren call, trying
to make the silicon chips smile at me and
bow to my innocent desire to play the
world's participation game.

To hell with progress.
To hell with cyberspace.
To hell with Pac Bell.

Most of all, to hell with this need I
have to be connected to something
that smiles and turns away, leaving
only a notice that there is an error in
my hard drive.

I don't need that.
I need acceptance.

Cranky

Opened my eyes this morning and
found myself swimming in thick stagnation.
Pulled the sheets over my head,
but the same despair was there.

Pushed my mummified body to the toilet.
Drained off some poisons. Looked in the mirror
and didn't care if I looked like shit.
A dangerous sign.

Wrapped myself in a thick green robe.
Sat quietly on the meditation pillow with legs
bent back and proceeded to find my life again.

Over and over I learn the same lesson:
If I want to breathe under water,
I have to sit very still and drown.

Just So

First you have to live a lot. Spend a number
of years attending to various aches and pains.
Undergo a few heartbreaks.
Suffer through several humiliating relationships.
Maybe get dumped and fish your self-esteem
out of the toilet once or twice at least.

There will be some falling on your knees
in gratitude for nanoseconds of understanding.
Then back to smiling through tight lips,
while the sorrow of human drama
locates itself just above your diaphragm.

Falling in love is a plus.
Having children will level you off.
Working to pay the bills, but nothing
extra, is sure to keep your heart tuned.
Good friends who pick you up at
the airport at midnight are essential.

When you have ripened in this way,
you may sit down, take your pencil in
hand, stare out the window a while,
empty your mind of all thoughts,
and finally receive the first draft
of something creative.
Perhaps a poem or a sacred moment of awe.

The mystery will decide what you receive.

The Ultimatum

The dollars in my wallet, keys in my pocket,
none of the usual ways will open the
storehouse where the wine is waiting.

At night I look up to heaven's necklace.
Morning brings Mother and I watch her
rise above the hills, sliding her gold into
my room, where there is only weeping.

So long I've pounded my own drum.
So many years I've folded my legs,
but still the door is locked from within.

I thirst. I starve.
I shuffle one day onto the other,
but only the telephone rings for me.

I tell you now, I will not settle for
anything less, only the sweetest wine.

This is just a fake life. I am not fooled.
I wait.

Love is the Answer

I operate within this flesh and bone.
I will have to die soon. The signs are very sure.
Even I can see my position is not the one to last.
I try to be aware and in control, but some large
emptiness carries every thought to obliteration.

Nothing I do, think or say survives.
I can become important, but never enough.
I am a temporary aberration in a vast, cloudless sky.
I shall not survive in this great not knowing.
That is the truth.

I can rage, and so I have.
I can weep, and so I have.
I can strategize, and so I have.
I can pray, and believe me, I have.
I can bargain with God, and so I have.
I can try to be a good man, and so I have.
I can make a family to survive me, and so I have.
I can take drugs and dance wildly, so I have.
I can meditate, be spiritual, to save myself.
You know I have.

Only love survives. I am wasting away in love.
The old clichés are true. Love is the answer
and the destination. It awakens us all from a strange dream.

So now I worship Love.
That's all there is.

Meditation on the true nature of mind reveals the many strategies we humans have for diversion. We work hard at finding ways to escape our dilemma. It's amazing how much attention we give to plans for solving what only appear to be problems.

Leaning Forward

When I lean forward to escape
the everything IS as it IS here,
I feel strain in my heart,
where real life lives.

Straining and thinking I must do
something, but thinking is not enough.

What is Here is obvious to anyone who slows down
enough to drop through a hole in time.
Into vast space, relaxation,
peaceful mind that sputters to a stop
for just a moment.

A mind that speaks without voice, believes nothing
and realizes in this ordinary moment,
we are all here.
Even when we look for a chance to escape.

I'm in a Hurry

I have so much to do!
Important tasks to cross off my list.
An endless need to accomplish.

If I continue without awareness,
If I keep speeding along my groove,
always looking into the distant future,
for what awaits to be done,
then,
I will never have to wake up
covered by dark thoughts of death
and meaningless work.

There is a hummingbird caught in the skylight.
She tries to fly towards the light.
She beats herself against the glass, until she falls from fatigue.

Wanting Creature

The wanting creature is loose!
All the time he leers and lurks
behind good thoughts and
desperate bursts of hope.

He corrals the unsuspecting,
surprises everyone with his
smart promises and chic ideas.

The wanting creature, born
within, living only to get out
and wreak violent greed.

Go after him! See where he hides
with all the wreckage dripping from
his fat and quivering jowls.
There is nothing to lose.
He has already destroyed
last year's crop.

He is no friend to anybody.
Only wants what feels good for
now and tells you that's all there is.

Don't believe him.
He'll trick you every time.
Then you'll have to start over again.

First, forgiveness.
Then the resolve to go on,
tip-toeing your way past his dark cave,
hoping today is the day he sleeps.
But you know deep down,
he is a very light sleeper.

Two Worlds

Tissue paper thin and moving in the wind of breath,
this membrane separating me from that other world,
where there is no longing, no separation, no other.

So close and yet beyond the reach of these solid bones,
this stubborn self baby, who reaches out of desire
instead of knowing.

In the meantime, I'll make some phone calls, get the paper,
have a coffee and walk around this world,
knowing that in the other one,
my footsteps are washed away by tides of light and sound.

Manual of Instruction

Reflect on yourself endlessly,
because *you* are all you have.
Those five senses will fail you
when the time to leave
bursts out like a surprise party.

Reflect on yourself until the edges blur,
until darkness closes in and your head disappears.
That's when some angel will come and gesture.

In the meantime be ordinary.
Putting in time is easy, if you
don't need to be anybody.

Sit at the table, drink your warm comfort,
be happy with friends, look at your fingernails,
open the mail, but all the while reflect on yourself.

It's a good sign
when you don't know
what to do next.
We don't have to go anywhere.

Wonderful Bird

This world is not a place to rest in.
Too much dissonance,
everything is eating everything here.
Life is pushing outward
gobbling creatures in the way.

All the horns are blowing.
Traffic is congested.
Drivers are leaning out their windows,
swearing at each other, shaking fists.

Everybody is attracted to something "other."
Repulsion follows attraction,
close behind.
Restlessness is everywhere.

I would like to declare an official time out,
make a tear in the membrane suffocating us.

We could shut our eyes and notice where
all the struggle comes from, inside here, where
the greedy one who wants to live pushes outward
like a river against a dam.

We could sense the joy that sings along
the surface of the river, like a wonderful
bird singing to God all day.

We could find the peace that comes
from sinking below the surface,
letting our opinions be carried
away like loose driftwood.

We could drift along together
having conversations in mid-stream,
flowing in the same direction, maybe side-by-side,
headed for the same beach, some distant shore.

The Narrow Path to Mystery

I am hopelessly human.
Obsession is my name.
Addiction is my nature.

Every day is filled with need.
I despise the wanting as though
it were alien other.

Every night is filled with loneliness
that comes from separation.
I cannot escape pornographic desire.

I slide my tongue along smooth thighs.
I gaze with lust on well-shaped buttocks.
I want the storekeeper to love me just
because I purchase his potatoes.

I worry about my children in a distant city.
I confess to friends my secrets,
so they will add their's to mine.

I scheme for money and sell my attention
for respect and payment in coins.
I walk through endless, thick sorrow,
despairing for some magic solution.

Finally, the torment of imagination,
The torture of uncontrolled dread
force me to a kneeling position.

At last, I take the narrow path that leads to peace,
crawl my way remembrance by remembrance,
decision by decision toward the swirling mystery
that begins it all.

Like the waves roll to the shore one after the other.
There is life here; I am that and worthy.
All creation floats in the movement of this mystery.
What I seek, I am.

Step by step, I cross the kitchen floor.
Increment by inch, I reach for the refrigerator door.
Muscle by tendon I walk into the garden where the roses are.

Arrogance Reveals Nothing

We have to surrender sometime.
Eventually there will be a wall for
butting heads and wailing.
Arrogance does not survive understanding.

I marched along making decisions
giving orders this way and that.
I knew what needed to be done
to satisfy ambition and desire.

I knew how to slay the dragon so
I could take the princess home.
Enlightenment was a matter of
bending dharma to my will.

Then, the flowers didn't smile in spring.
The song of love and beauty became a dirge.
The wall of black stone appeared before me
and every moment was diseased.

I cannot bring the breath.
I cannot beat the heart.
I cried.
Voices calling in the corridors
of the human brain do not owe
their power to me.

My arrogance reveals nothing but illusion.
Only on my knees can I see over that dark wall.

Only with tears can I see
the light that shines through failure.

Drinking Kindness Cup

Trungpa called it primordial dot.
That spot of presence before thinking
unrolls like a vast scroll in the sky.
He said it was good before good and evil.
Just good because it is. No question. No doubt.

No matter what person is involved, even
those who kill out of hatred have it stuffed
away somewhere inside.
Before the confused voices and raucous
screaming, we all have it: primordial dot.
You can count on it.

You can find it when you feel the worst of the worst.
Some kind of built-in radar beam to guide us all to
harmlessness and happiness.
We can be happy when we rest, relax and trust that spark of
light enough to sacrifice every treasure.

Throw away the collectibles.
Enter through the tiny doorway into big welcome home.
Where you been so long? Sit down.
Take a load off and have a cup of kindness.

Anyone who sits in meditation long enough will eventually encounter a deep fear of loss, which is our vivid discomfort with the truth of constant change. We yearn for security, but only find the shifting ground of appearance.

I Touch My Thigh

I touch my thigh.
It isn't young anymore.
Flesh is soft and without edges.
Getting ready to dissolve into old age.
Preparing to fall away from the bone.

I don't know what happens to us.
We are bright stars, full of brilliance.
Then, without notice, we become
inhabitants of decaying houses.
The transition tests our wisdom.

Arising and passing away,
expanding and contracting,
victims of some universal rule.
No apology for all the unmet expectations.

I touch my thigh.
Soft and not elastic.
I don't remember it to be that way.
Something has happened to this poor body.
It loses form, like fresh baked bread,
has no respect for my dismay.

No escape from liver spots and wrinkles,
joint pains and memory collapses.
Just part of the common day.

This body is getting old.

Broken down, weather-washed barns
in fields of golden grasses,
old photographs of skinny men in
tank tops at the beach.
Skeletons in unmarked graves.
Time is relentless and flesh is temporary.

Everything is coming and going,
Here one moment, gone the next.

One World • Different Beings

I could hardly believe what I saw,
standing next to the fuscia bush.
A full grown buck with antlers and
brown pools of gentleness
gazing at the world.

He stood there like an imaginary
magic messenger from the world of
mythic beasts.
We looked at each other in stillness.
Different species, yet interested.
Flies buzzed around his nose.

Later, while he moved on to the rose bush, I sat in
my studio talking with Judith who was beginning to
realize the truth of her mother's impending death.

While he gazed at us, munching on rose leaves,
Judith held her head, sobbing over the horror of separation.

I watched through the window as he turned away,
flicked his whisk-like tail, and walked
like one noble-born towards the apple tree.

Judith looked up and saw him leaving,
smiled through her tears.
I said, "You've been in denial of your
mother's leaving."

Always the therapist working in the
center of mystery, watching how the
ordinary becomes so shining new.
"Yes," she said, "I don't want her to die."

Buddha Life

What amazes me is the one who sits here releasing
these words into the world of bread and time.
He is quite aware of himself moving his fingers and
thinking deep thoughts now and then,
but he is also appearing simultaneously in some
Buddha life that has no agenda about doing stuff,
that just happens to be present when the familiar guy
answers the phone, heats up some soup, and climbs
the stairs at night to find rest from all his doing.

Buddha life is present and peaceful.
Buddha life is without question.
Always reliable, always available and never blaming.
He's full of joy over everything and neither desires,
expects nor rejects. He's guaranteed and trouble free.
Each day I understand him more.

Today I listened to a dying woman's complaints
about my failure to understand her pain.
I understood her complaints without apology.
Later I will walk out on the street and feel my
body walking in reality.

The moon still lingers, even though the day is bright. The
weather unusually warm.
Everything is altogether and here.
Myself included.

Only the Author Remains

The old man sits in the sun, contented,
watching everybody passing by.

The boy runs up the path and
rolls around on the living room floor.

The teacher sits before the class and
leads inspirations of the mind,
lessons of the soul.

The man exercises his body, stretches
the muscles and pumps the lungs.

The father visits his children,
approves of all they've been and
celebrates their children too.

Many people dance their way out of one body
during a single lifetime.
Many come and go. Some stay.

The body is the stage.
Many actors peek out from
behind the same pair of eyes.

Sometimes, in a single afternoon,
there will be changes of the cast.
Some are angry. Some are sad.
Some last a lifetime.

Others finish before sixteen.

When that spacesuit made of
flesh descends into its final
countdown, they all exit and seek
their author.

Death is common to us all.
It comes to the boy, the father,
the teacher and the actor.

Only the author remains—the one
who never reveals the end of the story.

Some Celestial Bell Somewhere

Does some celestial bell somewhere
sound a tone for our sorrows?

Is there finally a reward for being
voiceless and helpless at the hour
before the sun rises?

We are so small here and
no one knows the other.
Split apart and longing for
shared lives and intimate sighs.

Is this really what it is?
I remember more, somehow,
and soothe my heart and wait
the return of love's easy breath.

A Touch of Freedom

Today we could walk around
behind thoughts into the
empty shining sky,
even though our feet feel solid.

We could look behind thoughts
and observe how experience
has never belonged to us,
not even the pain nor the breath.
Not even the sound of thinking
nor the desire to be free.

Surrender. It's not so bad.
We won't lose anything, only gain a
wise moment in a life that drifts
from day to day
without a stone to hold it down.

We think, but thinking isn't what's real.
It's so hard to know the truth.
We have to sit very still and be in wonder,
perhaps wait and receive on our tongues
a thin wafer of understanding.

Eventually, we get fed, nourished
and then the mystery carries us away.

On Returning Home after a Long Time Away

The clematis bush is overgrown a bit.
The yellow brick path to the veranda
seems as warm as always.
A glance around the garden,
things look good, especially the begonias.

Unlocking the kitchen door
should be accompanied by
celestial orchestras.

To have a solid home on this
constantly melting earth is a
comfort, a blessing.

Home welcomes the lonely heart,
wandering back from working in the fields.
Its sweet spirit soothes jet-lagged wounds.
The body shuffles fatigued through the happy
doorway into memories of a life well lived.

I clear the cobwebs and make room for more memories.

Dark Days

When we are hungry, who will feed us?
Is there nourishment enough for all the
open mouths when times are dark like these?

Are there storehouses of faith?
Is hope in large supply?
Will bliss be abundant sometime soon,
before it's time to die?

Hard rain is falling now.
Crops not doing well.
The people are hiding low.
Stories they tell are not sweet.

Across the fields, homeless refugees
come crawling, stricken faces, sunless air,
afraid their flesh will freeze.

Who will bring them supper?
Who will feed them praise?
The times are shattered terribly.
The future brings dark days.

Pray God there be some mercy.
That light will be preserved.
That songs still live in sadness
and punishment be deserved.

Mindfulness of the Body

Let's stand in the mud and watch
our legs sink in organic matter.
Squish the stuff between our
toes, make pies with our hands,
roll around with our clothes off
getting dirty with earth.

The only time peace comes,
no strain, total satisfaction, is
when we fall out of concepts
into flesh. Here and now.

Let's sit down in the barnyard.
Smell the manure.
Watch the moisture drip from the velvet
noses of placid cows.
Their eyes so beautiful and brown.

When ideas arrive, let's not believe they are
more real than an itch between the shoulders.
That way, we'll all be here together
living in the same time.

What Really Counts

I was just sitting there and nothing happened.
For once there were no voices,
no planning, no Technicolor memories.
Whatever drives the thinking machine
had taken a break.
Left to run the company was
an empty desk, no papers.
No telephone to ring.

It's hard to describe the simplicity of sitting
without agenda and no past to speak of.

Sometimes they call it emptiness,
but it was full of life and wonder.
When neurosis skips a beat,
you can see forever through the
crack in your mind.

I was just sitting there.
The one who wants something
all the time was absent.
The ordinary revealed.
Ordinary body-life.
Soft white light.
Relaxation.
The sound of presence.
The stuff that lives so sweetly
Behind the struggle to be human.

Hymn to Space

Dirigibles and airplanes
make their swift descents
without concern for those who fly them.

Space holds us firmly even when falling.
The man across the street, used to perform barrel
rolls in his little piper cub. He never fell too far.

Our arteries harden, but we can fly
through the mind's barriers.
We don't have to know
where we are going all the time.

Big space holds all the ups and downs.
We can walk around in it, or let go and plunge
through it, but it never lets us down.

Just think how trees, and birds, and
stones all have their place.
Sometimes moving, sometimes not.
No one is going anywhere really.

For everywhere we go space
enfolds us, holds us safe.
Perhaps we should turn 'round and
'round with our arms out,
dance to all the music everywhere.

There is music in the air.

Gratitude for What is Here

There is only one of everything.
Only one sky and one beginning,
one life shared by so many.

No matter where I look, the obvious
circle of participants have no idea
where they come from, but all
assume the truth of being here.

When I pass the auto repair shop
down the street, the blond mechanic
in greasy overalls says hello.
The man who stands on the corner
watching traffic grunts sometimes,
but I know he is just shy.

The people at the post office either
greet me or not.
I lift the coffee cup from the table at the
deli and look through the window at life
moving in so many ways, and realize
again, we are all being moved and we take
it for granted.

It would be good to bow our heads in gratitude.

All at Once

The garden is lovely today.
Kissed by hummingbirds.
Watered yesterday and fresh like my
grandfather's cellar with its moist walls,
its smell of inland lakes and old toads sitting
on the steps near the cider barrels,
filled with his special apple brew.

The garden and childhood memories,
the here and now, songs of birds— none of it
excludes my sitting here nursing a sore back,
gazing out of a window towards the trees.

I wait for the next line, empty of words,
only able to catch some image on the fly and
wrestle it onto paper where it will speak to
someone or catalyze an expression of bafflement.

All I intended was to share
something of my heart with anyone
interested enough to be patient and take
some moments to hear a gesture from deep
within this body surrounded by a lovely garden
filled with sunlight and hummingbirds.

Happiness and You

Health is happiness.
Happiness is health.
Why settle for less?

Now, there is something I have to confess:

I sit in the middle.
I pay attention to now.
I feel all the troubles and never know how.

But something Big here keeps happening
without my assist. The river keeps
flowing, even when I resist.

Let go into nothing.
Lay down all your arms,
we never are happy when sounding alarms.

Life is exciting, overwhelming at least.
Surrender your opinions,
Calm your wild beast.

Happy is healthy, and
comes with let-go.
Remember your self here.
Nothing else is to know.

Lay down your objections, recover your mood,
your attitude toward presence is also your food.

The entire journey can be described as the process of returning our attention, again and again and again from the internal discussion ABOUT our lives to the vivid experience of here and now. That way, we learn about the reality of things.

In a Moment

The sun is shining
through the doorway.

A fly zigzagging its way
around my coffee cup,
when the beloved brushes
so sweetly against my mind.

The voices of other
people in the room ring hollow.

Someone is crying
in the distance:

"I don't know what to do!
I don't know what to do!"

I turn my heart's attention
inward and say,

"I'll stay here with you.
I'll stay here with you."

The Endless Present

We are always going somewhere,
heading out toward the distant
peak, buying camels to carry us
across some desert of the mind,
landscape of the soul.

I can't find a place to go.
I've been preparing for some voyage
for a long time but, now, there isn't any path
and I'm sitting on this rock with my maps.

The light comes and goes.
Sometimes it is night.
I eat and drink what's given.
I think about what I'm doing here.
I close my eyes and notice
the voyage comes to me.

A river of wonders wells up out
of the darkness and, sitting still, I
become memories.
I swim in emotions that have the
power of fire and water.
I am washed with the movement
of some infinitely joyous,
endlessly appearing thing.

I sit here, then, in wonder when
all the places come to me and

there is nothing to attain, leaving
me lost and satisfied upon this rock.

What is a goal, where is a
destination, who is traveling
 there, and what is the expected
time of arrival?

Death will come to us whether
we move or remain in the same
small room.

And death is the biggest surprise of all.
It doesn't come from the future and never
travels to the past. For when we die, the
endless present has arrived at last.

The Cycle of Being

Two roses in the garden,
one is white, one is yellow.
They hang on their thorny
stalks waiting for the sun to
burn petals to brown.

Petals fall onto the summer
soil and settle into the matter
of time and decompose into
earth and fire—then when
water is added it transforms the
elements of reality into beauty.

Food for the roots of life that
have been sprawled under the
surface, while the whole time
life and death danced through
their amazing concert.

Song

Whisper to me in the dark of the night.
Send me some pick-me-up and make it all right.

I'll sit on my cushion, notice my breath
and for a while forget about death.

Yea, doolie doolie. Yea, doolie doolie doo.
I'll sit quietly and listen for you.

Take your place in my brain cells.
Fill the space in my heart, can't do much
myself, but talking this stuff could be a start.

I'm just a poor doofus here all alone,
nobody can know me so throw me a bone.

Yea, doolie doolie. Yea, doolie doolie doo,
I'm happy to be here when you're here too.
I'm happy to be here when you're here too.

Before the Questions Come

Before the questions come,
before doubt visits and spreads
its infection, there is a
consciousness reserved for
brilliant clarity and very subtle
smiles, the kind you see on
statues of Siddhartha after he
received the holy touch.

I want to live there always in that
empty limitless, where intuition
is all that moves my mind and
guides the way my hands move,
my mouth speaks and where my
feet will walk upon this Earth
and with whom. Oh, isn't that
devoutly to be wished?

When I stop wishing I could live there,
in that state where nobody is around to make an effort . . .
when I stop wishing it were so,
and notice the music around my head,
the trees dancing with the blue emptiness
of limitless sky right before my eyes . . . .
Then I know I've always been at home.
Isn't that a mystery?

Before the questions come, before doubt
even becomes a thought in the mind.

No Great Notion

Sometimes I am an empty vessel, waiting for words.
Being empty is like having nowhere to go and nothing
to do, just feeling the presence of that, which could be
anything. There are, of course, many impulses to lurch
into activity, but they are bare stirrings with no
particular purpose except to initiate something.

I don't know why there is this resistance to emptiness,
but I can witness thoughts about life that seem to want
to stir something up, some drama, some story to
believe in. I am not interested in having a purpose.
I am not moved by my big adventure. I am willing to
stay with not this, not that. Nothing is interesting, but
I'm not bored. I have no point of view.

People talk to me, but I have nothing to say. I listen.
I witness lives being lived. I honor suffering for what
it is. I see so much tragedy. Gratitude would be better
for everybody. Being without self is lovely.
There is something coming into being every moment.
I call it energy, but it is really life.

Whoever writes these words doesn't know what they mean.
I will get up from my desk in a moment, go downstairs and fill
time with complication, letting ordinary stuff be important.
Return to emptiness is vacation—peace of mind.

Beyond the Layer of Grief

Down past the layer of grief,
there is a doorway to God.
Sinking below the tears, no longer
straining to see ahead, no longer
waiting for bandits.
The whole journey is an episode of letting go.

Laughter fills my mind.
The wanting creature remains
slavering in his cave.
No matter how many times
I descend past the valley of grief,
there's really no way to be,
other than me.

So let's get on with it!
Thaw out the frozen lunches.
Wipe the sweat away, and let my eyes shine in the dark.
There is time to spend and troubles to create in this world.
We are on a mission, and it doesn't help to rob each other.

We are here together to be life arising.
Out of the mysterious place of arising.
Passing through the doorway to God,
beyond the layer of grief, like a torrent of
sensations into this present breath
where I am so happy to be making these noises.

I am so happy to be here today with you.

The Torrent

If you sit very quietly,
you will eventually notice
a torrent of life-stuff pouring
toward you, entering into your heart,
breaking through the uppermost gates,
filling all your empty reservoirs,
carrying on its foaming crest sure
wisdom, heart food, and kinship
with all the trees.

The silent Earth will bear testimony.
The sitting body will be the portal,
offering its head and heart to be in union
with the Great Mind that thinks all things.

There is nothing to build, everything is already in place.
So open the sluice gates, release the contracted heart.
Listen carefully, like you would listen for your assassin.
Hear the presence of life itself filling what you call your own,
replacing struggle, substituting happiness for fear.

That power, that wild river, will rush
into all your hidden corners,
transform itself to rapture when
you see what has come to visit is
simply everything you are.
Making you divine, another member
of the human race, belonging to the
species, everything that lives.

Map of Being

No matter how I do it,
there is always return to mystery.

One thought swoops out of nothingness,
another follows, colors, lines, memories and
conversations, worries about body health,
pictures of faces, even down to moles and
freckles then emptiness again.

There is nothing in emptiness. Really empty.

Then another thought pops up, moves around
gathering attention, scooping up energy in order
to get real somehow.
They pour out of nowhere, tumbling over each other.

The body is like that too. First a
shoulder, then the belly and of course
the pelvis, and behold the feet,
the thumbs and an ache, a vibration,
a feeling of warmth.

The process, the creative movement
happens with us or without us.

Ordinary Life

Wooden spoon standing in the kitchen all this time.

Long slender and useful, always there when needed,
made of the essence of tree, bringing that tree into my house,
not the roots nor the bark, but the spirit of the thing.

A piece of the original idea, like ourselves,
just fragments of some large trunk.

Here

Here is where the heart is.
Here is upside-down and sideways
never holding still, always careening
to the light, always pulsing with
the sound of everything arriving.

Here we are in this movie,
characters undergoing torment,
running around in our clothes,
all designed to make us happy.
We are throwing our heads back in laughter,
hoping to make our flesh feel better.

Here plants grow and children grow
and teachers tell us to be careful because
the end is coming and we don't know about it,
but we don't know about anything.
Here we are improving our personalities.

Here is where the ego-eating machine
does its work, scrapes the holy presence clean
of all desire to possess what it just produced.
Oh, here is a miracle too astounding to be witnessed
by we who are fascinated with being here.

Here is the place of glory, where the source of all things bursts
into full bloom and drops its seeds everywhere.
Here is the time of awakening, a distant drum beating cadence,
calling us out of ourselves to be here.

Spreading the Word

We are afraid to be happy.
Tremulous about getting the news.

We are afraid to step into our
new clothes, walk in sturdy shoes
and let our faces shine.
Afraid someone will object to
our celebration.

Perhaps we will step on
someone's toes while dancing
through our transformation.

But I am in flight like an eagle.
My wings are wisdom and love.
My feathers are thoughts of well-being.

I will soar over the deserts and beaches
calling loudly for all to hear.
Can you hear my screeching?

I am clearly here.

The Seeker

Four times the trumpets blew.
Four times the observers turned
their heads like in a tennis match.

In the swamps, the water fowl
lifted off with their great wings,
but still the Seated One remained
immobile, enlightened, smiling
slightly, as though waiting for
history to make statues of Him
sitting there while everything
continued around Him.

I was jealous.
I wanted not to wonder
what four times meant or
who those observers were.

I could appreciate the flying waterfowl,
but I was caught in linear thought and
couldn't smile as easily as He did.

I'll sit and practice some more.

The Sweetest Presence

Rain washes the trees in my garden.
They sway and bow gracefully.
Grey winds and mists of moisture wrap
around my house like cashmere blankets.
My heart, like the trees,
is full of gratitude for this life.

I have visited the holy temple within
and discovered darkness, light and
sweet sounds.
I have moved the bones and flesh of
this body into difficult shapes and
breathed deeply into fountains of
dramatic sensations.

Now, I make note of what I believe.
Perhaps, later, when I read this
poem over a cup of tea or a glass of
wine, my heart will open again in
remembrance of times spent in
communion with the rain,
the trees, my body, a million thoughts
and the sweetest presence surrounding
all of them, all of us, everywhere, always.

Some days, everything makes sense without struggle.
Some days we have to remember that it once did
and will again.

Wedding Song

When two of us by some miracle
are able to see each other,
feel, taste, smell, and become
free enough to touch, then draw
around ourselves that translucent
bubble called "being in love,"
the whole world rejoices.

Once again a chance, an opportunity
arises for all us fragments of divinity
to rest from striving to surrender our separate
sufferings and truly feel the vibrating flesh,
joyful gift of holy life itself.

When two of us join together to remember our
divinity in that way, we all ascend.
We all awaken in the lover's bed.

Gradually, we learn to let go of all the habitual ways we have of contracting against life. When we give up the search, surrender our battle positions, the great mystery of wholeness reveals itself. What bliss, to discover how interconnected our world is.

Within the Body You are Wearing

Within the body you are wearing, now,
inside the bones and beating in the heart,
lives the one you have been searching
for so long.

But you must stop moving and shake hands.
The meeting doesn't happen without your presence,
your participation.

The same one waiting for you
there is moving in the trees,
glistening on the water, growing
in the grasses
and lurking in the shadows you create.

You have nowhere to go.
The marriage happened long ago.
Behold your mate.

I Don't Know • Do You ?

Reason doesn't have much to do with it.
I can sit down and think I'm actually
busy making things happen, but no
control over who or what gets born.

Some giant intelligence turns and turns.
While those of us who think we are the one
thinking are reminded at every turn about the
source—how tomatoes are red,
how we don't know who is talking
or whether to write it down or not.

I love being a piece of material goods
talking to myself all the time about how
strange and wonderful life is.

I know I'm being carried in my little boat,
ever closer to the waterfall—the ultimate thrill.
Maybe I'll finally submit my ideas on how
this all works back into the vast emptiness from
which my arms, legs, head, belly, genitals,
longings, dreams, cries, poems and prayers
                              e-m-e-r-g-e so mysteriously.

Forgiveness

Thousands of times I've wished for redemption
and the easy breath that comes with forgiveness
of sins, real or imagined.

But where does one find that blessing?
Certainly not from moralists who carry
the book around in their hearts,
nor from pious posers who hide their
shame inside splendid robes.

But always from the place holding truth
within the darkest darkness,
lying under softest moss, surrounded by the
sweetest trees, in the most intimidating forest
of confusion guarding the heart's gate.

Where to enter is given only
to the most courageous body,
full of gratitude, kindness,
generosity, given freely to the
sinner and the child who
reside in all of us who seek
belonging in the family of
conscious love.

Metaphysical Meandering

The storekeeper,
the postmistress,
the family of quail in my garden
evading the yellow tabby who visits everyday.

The kitchen door opens onto
warm sights and smells.
The veranda's skylights catch
unwitting hummingbirds.
The mail in post office box 378, the thoughts in my mind,
the words that tumble out of my mouth are all
lost in space and time.
The asphalt road behind the high hedges,
the very light surrounding all this; so much stuff,
so many forms and concepts,
the world is full of events and things.

We look for the ultimate stuff. We want to know the
common denominator, but we live at the end of emptiness
where everything arises in time,
pours forth into our laps, fascinates us until we are
weighed down, no longer able to get up.

Let's open our eyes, stretch and scratch,
take some deep breaths, and wake up to see how it all comes
from nowhere and shines brightly for a moment or two,
then disappears like images on a
television—nowhere to be found.

Message to My Divine Lover

How many times will you reject
me before I tear out your heart
and eat it bloody?

Do you think this game can be
played forever?
Not so! I have other admirers to
attend to!
So get me N-O-W while I'm hot.

I won't always need your sweet smell.
I won't forever swoon under your kisses.
This driving need to be consumed
by you could be gone by morning.

And then I'll leave your precious ass and thighs
to fend for themselves, all tangled in after-love sheets.

How many times do you think
my heart can be broken?

You are not the first you know.

Gratitude

When that little sperm fellow goes
chasing after sweetheart egg,
little do they both know about the
big picture.

When hydrogen and oxygen first start
rubbing up against each other,
they don't do it so we can have a drink
of water.

The sun and moon turn their ways
around open space but they aren't
concerned about the delicate balance.

I look at you and wonder how I ever
moved this life along the track
it took all these years, before you
opened your eyes in my doorway and
smiled like gardenias.

When I see us together, the idea of
wholeness takes birth in new form.
Now I breathe because you do.

Now I look at the world and see
perfection where there used to be
gaping wounds.

Rumi

I am longing to love like Rumi.
To throw my heart on the ash heap in frenzy,
daring the beloved to pick it up,
hold it close and break this loneliness.

Although I have ridden the dawn horse of renewal,
I have yet to give my head to the chopping block.
I have yet to pull out the last roots,
dark shadow in my blessed body.

I long for a love that takes hold of my life
with tentacles of desire and stops every
movement, except the arm and arm walking
toward luminous laughter, head to head secrets.

I want to be thrown to the ground,
stricken dumb by the silver rays that flash
from that kind of lover's eyes.
I want to want nothing but the lover's presence.

I want to crawl on my belly.
I want to dance on the balls of my feet,
then find myself on my knees not knowing
how such a force came upon me,
like the explosion of a vessel in the brain.

Such a love is all the meaning to be hoped for.
Such a love makes the very breath a gift
from the beloved.

I'll sit now in this corner, fold my legs, and
wait until the hand is placed upon my head.

And that lover, who has all the colors and all the
music woven into his clothes, sits beside me,
whispers the same prayer and laughs aloud at the
way my mind twists itself out of shape.

I know that lover is waiting for me to notice.

Prophecy

I have prophecy.
There will be orange marmalade.
There will be romantic songs at breakfast.
There will be sunscreen for every bald head.
There will be a spirit guide for every occasion,
and the rivers will run with rose water.

There will be a day when all us humans sit
down to lunch and everyone will realize
we have always been sitting down to eat.

I can see into the future.
Dinner will be delight.
No cows will have to die and
lambs will leap with safety.
Candlelight everywhere.
Lips will look redder and fuller,
hair will be pleasantly brightened,
eyes will shine with expectation,
fulfillment only a breath away.

I can know the times to come.
Our hearts will open like white roses
and our bodies will be vases of beauty.
We will still have to brush our teeth and
clean our fingernails, wash out our ears.
All the necessary things done easily like
tying our shoes, touching others gently,
tying up the garbage and carrying it to the curb.

I have prophecy.
Our hearts will open gently to
each other and we will know all
the thoughts, be able to keep the
ones that make us dance.
Trust the winds. Salute the sun.
Lay our hands gently on the earth.
Say our gratitude to the great
Mother—that Big Mama.

The Living Body

It's important to find our freedom
in this living body.
Bring in the humerus and the
thigh bone, the large intestine
and the cervical vertebrae.
Bring all the parts together in one place.

We have to let the body be whole,
enjoy the Earth and smile with real
affection for each other.
How good to move our arms in circles
and feel the strength to stand.

To know how feet are made to
walk upon the ground and
how they spread to meet the
Earth's support.

How good to arch our backs
and let our faces turn upward,
throats open to sing!

Stomp the feet and move in dances.
Swing the arms and lift the knees up high.
Feel the warmth along the spine.
The life force there will never die.

Song of the Unborn

I sing of nothing.
About the sweetness
and freedom there.

I sing of emptiness.
The joy and lightness
of being therc.

Nothing. Emptiness.
The place of potential
where all our dreams
and notions come from.
Before the movement
of trees in the wind.
Before the movement
of legs and arms.

Only the unborn dances
with the music that lives
beyond the mind.

I sing of nothing.
The garden where we
bloom and never die.

Autumn Whimsy

So be it.
The leaves have started to fall
from those apple trees in the garden.
There are baby mice in the pantry
eating into sacks of rice and
shitting on the shelves.

What is this emptiness out of
which everything happens?
What is this mystery so
indifferent to joy and sorrow?

The mornings are crisp now. Soon the
fires will be lit to warm up the cave.
Days are getting shorter.

How do we know when a life has been
lived to the hilt?
How to scan some sixty years and
pronounce them well spent, a loving
heart well used?
Has the effort been enough,
the job well done?

Perhaps we should never ask
those questions, only say,
"So be it," and watch the days
get shorter, the nights longer
and the mystery deepen.

The Final Cut

I can hear you coming.
Suddenly, when thoughts stop
there you are.
I listen to the thread of connection in the
center of your sound.

You fill me up.
You appear from all sides.
Then, when the struggle ceases,
you enter me like a soft mood and fill me
with your nourishing food.

You never fail me. It isn't your way.
You serve. You serve, that's what you do.
Carrying me farther to where the sun lives, and
everything that arises out of you is blessed.

You are the music that connects us all.
You are the sound of love in a baby's ears.
You are comfort and safety and lush gardens.
You are unspeakable and present, always.

Why do we wander around in this dense darkness
so long, when you are so near our heads?
What is this story, always unfinished and full of tears?
Do we stumble here on rocky ground in order to find you?

Tear me apart with your sound!
Rip open my heart and pour in your healing liquid!

Remind me every moment of your ownership.
I'm only waiting for you to make the final cut.

Or will the end be just the beginning and
the cut more of a caress from deep within?
I don't need the answers to any questions.
Just come and do your melting business now.

I can only live in you.
There is no air to breathe elsewhere,
no place where you are not.

So let's do it!
Take me away one more time.

The mystery of union, of awakening beyond the mere appearance of things, brings the reality of love and devotion. We are filled with gratitude for the happiness that comes from seeing clearly.

When I Work in the Fields

I work in the fields all day and cry for you at night.
You eventually come. In the morning you come.
When I collect this body, your vessel, and hold it still,
you come and pour yourself into this pitcher.

You caress my eyes. Your lips
touch mine, when only my lips
touch each other.

Your sound announces your coming.
This head opens to your light.
These eyes untie themselves, relax, and
every cavity, from thorax to belly, fills with you.

I go into the fields. I take you with me.
I let you do the work.
There is nothing more for me to do,
just listen to you.
Listen to you, listen to you, bringing the
voices of many people, a cup of tea,
a friend, bringing the post office and the storekeeper
and a sandwich at the deli,
with dark French roast.

How did I ever deserve this blessing?
The vessel is dirty and still you fill it with yourself.
I break my promises to you every day.
In the morning you are there.

I stumble through the day, never knowing how,
and you guide my hands and steady my heart.
Birds are singing and dancing on the air
outside my window.

I pause, hear your presence in this brain, and
go about the business of the day.

You came again this morning.

My Teacher

My teacher is always changing her clothes.
My teacher is here one minute, there the next.
No guarantee about the daffodils in spring,
nor the snowfall in December.

My teacher blows her breath and creates the
wind, farts and turns the swamps to miasma.

Just behold how it happens all around us,
now and now and now, this and then this.

My teacher is the appearance of the divine
One in the movement of every insect and the
barking of all the dogs.

My arms move, my feet crave the earth
because my teacher speaks to me all down
the days, stormy or vanishing in golden
California sunlight.
My teacher is the One who turns the planets
like children play with tops.

Just see how all the trees dance for her.
Notice now the appearance of her masterpiece.
There is no greater one and, yet,
she bends and touches me with respect.

The Real Teacher

The real teacher is inside.
The real teacher is climbing around
in the trees and on the mountains.

The real teacher is moving our fingers.
The real teacher is one of a kind, rolling with our
thoughts and spinning cloth out of emotions.

The real teacher is inside and
bursting out everywhere, turning
sunny days into hurricanes, shaking
the Earth until the bridges fall down.

The outside and inside are like life and death,
faces on the coin, sides of the whole, and
the Mother-Father-God is birthing us all
without a rest, whether we witness the miracle or
lie sleeping all curled up inside our tents.

The real teacher is inside and everywhere.
Let's rejoice in That One. Sing songs, dance wild dances,
and touch each other with love.
The moon is visible at night, the sun at day,
always there for us to celebrate.

The Man Said

The man said, "Love one another."
The man said, "Do what needs to be done."

Those were the instructions.
Passed down through many lives.
Spoken by mouths that moved in times
before we flew on metal wings and traveled
on soft wheels.

Simple, no frills.
My teacher told me to go with what's obvious.
Simple, no frills.

So here I sit and there is breathing.
So here I sit and there is movement.
Warmth, pressure, light, color.
Simple joy, only sitting, appearing here, this body,
these thoughts, no need to remember anything.

Thank you for the opportunity.
Thank you for the pleasure,
the pain also.
Gratitude, praise, humility, respect.
No struggle for the moment.

Another breath has been given.
Another miracle received.
More of the same life.
Always fresh, appearing out of

this mystery that is all of us.

Earth, Air, Fire, Water, and a mind that thinks
all things, doing what needs to be done.

The man said, "Love one another."
The man said, "Do what needs to be done."

The Meditators

There is this sensation and that thought.
We pay attention to them, make
sure we know which is which. We do that don't we?
We sit carefully, like the cat before the mole-hole.
We are witnesses to all kinds of pain and pleasures. Sometimes
we witness life just the way it is.

And then, there is that mystery around everything.
The deep echo that appears for an instant.
The never-ending possibility, the place
our bones come from. Do we name it, too?
Some just call it THAT, and include
the stones and whispers, too.

Great void, womb of all attention and
all objects disappearing.
We co-exist, you and I. Who is who?
I'm this one with the heart softly yearning.
I worry about doing the right thing and ask endlessly.
I search for love with every step and despair frequently.

You, oh you, what do you do but give birth all night and day?
You are the hall the party celebrates itself within.
You are the big question and the ultimate answer,
the music all the lyrics sing within.
I am your brother and your sister. I am twins, torn in two.
You are the nothing I am identical to.
What a mystery! What a love story! What a play!
Thank you, Thank you, Thank you, every day.

Fine-Tuning

I am fine-tuning my axons,
dendrites and neurons to
your wavelength's vibration so my
brain will be an extension of your grace.

This brain will be a radio receiver,
shortwave transformer of all your
information, all your heart-food,
all your thrilling leaves and flowers.

I am fine-tuning my brain for you
to come in clearly, an SOS, an SOS.
Do your hear me? I want to become
your transmitter, the conduit of your
eternal sound, your special holy riff.
I am so happy to do that.

I am your street sweeper,
radio-repair-man.
I am in your union and we are all on STRIKE!

Send Me a Message

Working my way home, that's the job.
It's a long time coming.
Working my way home.
I'm tired.
Will you come to me, even though
I haven't cleaned my boots and
need a shave?

Send me a message if you can't come in person.
Let me know you are clocking my track,
that you see the way I pull against the wind.
Send me one of those wordless letters you do so well,
just at the last moment. I need one soon.
My knees don't work anymore.
They don't bend enough, and my feet are on backwards.

Working my way home, that's the business here.
But I have to finish everything on the table,
before having nothing is possible.
Having nothing, the place where you play that music,
the blues mixed with a sweet violin.

You can afford to let me know it's alright.
Send me a message. You know the kind I want.
My feet are covered with chains, now, and
each step is full of the promise of joy.

Send me a message.
I'm working my way home.

Holy Fax

I am the airwaves.
I am the movement of insects and birds.
I am what happens before birth.
I am the sound before words.
I am the movement of thought.

There is only where I come from and
that place is no place for I am before
space, and time is only the
measurement of my beauty.
I am before anything is and
what everything becomes.
Out of me is the Holy Child.

When you listen, you can hear me.
When you receive on your tongue,
you can taste me. I am what you feel.
There is no limit to my happiness and
no bottom to my sorrow.

No walls imprison me and no
freedom sets me free, for I am
already the inside and the outside.
Look for me anywhere and I will be what
you see before color and line become form.
I am unexplainable.

Screams are in me.
Walks along the sea.

Forests are in me, the stars as far as you can see.
Baskets of flowers, hammers and nails,
carpenters and their smiles.
Windows and blades of grass, shoelaces,
ice skates, rivers, canals and fires in lonely
caves, fur blankets and daisies, pinups,
staples, Wall Street, coal mines and rockets.

I am the one that thoughts drift within.
Everyone knows who I am.

Pleasure Seeker's Prayer

I am a secret pleasure seeker and everyone knows it.
I want all the flavors, sighs, shivers, and every moment of
delight that could possibly slosh its way through this
bag of water, this wonderful flesh arrangement.

Give it all to me and, when the time
for gratitude prayers comes,
let me sit in a dark corner and pull
the blessed comforter over my head,
so alive with shooting stars.

Let me tell you of my love for you who
brings it all with just a movement of your
divine compulsion to create this
electronic virtual reality everything that
IS.
Oh, I love you and I hope you know it.
I can only bow my head to show it.

Happiness is Free

We never know when happiness will strike.
Just like the way the heart beats and
the lungs fill with food for life,
those bubbles of champagne delight
appear out of nowhere and
ripple up our grateful vertebrac
as though they have always been there
and those long dreary dreamlike days of
gray sadness never happened.

The wait is worth it.
But wouldn't it be nice if the interval
between despair and being awake
could shrink like time does when happiness
makes all the clocks useless?

Facing Facts

The world is a vast prison.
I know because I've been outside,
where the cloak of separation
no longer wraps around some spirit
that cries for freedom, but can't
remember long enough to rest in peace.

This world is a trap,
a maze leading only into solid walls
of limitation and frustration.
There is a path to open air,
but to actually stride there,
requires more courage than
anybody has a right to.

Stop trying to get free!
Give up the desperation.
Let them come and get you
when your time is up.
No one knows how long
we have to serve.

We only have what is here.

The Mansion

This mansion where we live has many rooms.
For most, the favorite hangout is the drama room,
sometimes called the place of stories.
Yesterday's conversations are retold there.
The wounds of childhood sleep deeply,
sit up wide-eyed from nightmares,
walk into the day and suffer from the replay,
prisoners of the past.

The drama room is fine for laughter, too.
Neurosis pulling at your sleeve and doing
floppy-hat routines, falling on the knees,
tap dancing across your screen in search of
applause or sympathy.
Everybody out to get even with somebody,
or waiting to fall in love.
There are seven basic plots that get redone
with endless variations for more fun.

The next room is where feelings happen,
 behind the story and just below the mind.
All the drama finds its way into the body,
pulls it this way, constricts it that.
Every meaningful glance, every jealous
moment sends its current through the nerves,
transforms itself to impulse, contracts the
muscles and pulls upon the bones.
In the feeling room, we pay attention to the
pressure of contraction, the connective

117

tissue, making its demand.

That leads us to the sensation room where
life happens in the raw. Opinions belong to
drama and plans are not allowed.
Sensations are acknowledged simply as they are.
Some are tingling some are pain, vibration travels
through in waves, touch recorded like falling rain.
No need to make them into something, no story here
to tell. Each stands alone and disappears, replaced by
what comes next, maybe heat, perhaps cold,
tightness, hardness, maybe the sense of presence,
familiar and so old.

Sensation without drama, presence without
history, no story to be told.
Sensations move like blinking stars.
The body has no form, no familiar
shoulders, no arms to make us warm.
Only life emerging now.
Insistent, demanding and ecstatic,
full of movement, abounding with power,
running behind the eyes and darting out the
fingertips, dissolving all identity, becoming
Isness, arriving Buddha nature,
the same as birds and song.
Making toast in the morning, head upon the
pillow in the night. Walking to the kitchen,
turning to the right, whispering to a lover,
the act of looking and the sight.

The mansion is the Great One.
We who live here are mirage.
Only the One Who Lives is here.
Smiling when the tea is hot, spreading on
the jam, bringing down the laundry, wiping
out the cooking pot.

How wonderful is this body.
How tender is the love.
We imagine we are separate,
but the truth is all around us,
below us and above.

Marvel

Where does it all come from?
We don't know.
We don't bring the breath
or the beating heart
or the inner sound of calling,
the constant reminder that we
are not permanent residents here
but collections of memories
and dancing elements
all on loan for the moment,
so that a sip of tea,
a deep sigh,
the bowels twisting in their cavern
are all events staged from some
clever screenplay written by nobody
and acted by no bald old man sitting
on a meditation cushion,
smiling at the sweetness of such generous
mystery, such wild imagining
beyond anything anyone ever thought
or decided to produce.

We are beautiful strands of amusement,
threads of momentary desire,
indescribable twists in the wind.